Wakefield Press

driving to mulberrygong

driving to Mulberrygong is the final collection of Adelaide poet Miriel Lenore (1928–2024), her selection from more than thirty years of writing. Some poems have never been published, some are long-time favourites.

The collection brings together themes arising from the writer's varied and adventurous life: country kid, botanist, researcher, traveller, student, teacher, activist, feminist, mother, grandmother. Miriel spent twenty years in Fiji, forty years in the Australian women's movement and the Adelaide writing scene, and ten years as a regular visitor to a Ngaanyatjarra community in the Western Desert.

Also by Miriel Lenore

Poetry

the Lilac Mountain (in Across the Gulf – with June Dally and Adele Kipping)
sun wind & diesel
travelling alone together (with Ruby Camp by Louise Crisp)
drums & bonnets
the Dog Rock
in the garden
a wild kind of tune
smoke
ties of silk

Performance

Masterkey (text, with Mary Moore, from Masako Togawa)

Some of the poems in *driving to Mulberrygong* have been published previously in various literary journals and anthologies including Australian Humanities Review, Cargo, foam:e, Four W, Friendly Street Reader, Hecate, Hobo, Jacket 2, LINQ, Otis Rush. Overland, PAN, Rippling Web, Science Made Marvellous, Southerly, Tarantella, The Australian Weekend Review, The Big Spoon (UK).

driving to mulberrygong

Miriel Lenore

Wakefield Press

Wakefield Press
16 Rose Street
Mile End
South Australia 5031
www.wakefieldpress.com.au

First published 2025

Text designed and typeset by Jesse Pollard, Wakefield Press

ISBN 978 1 92338 803 1

A catalogue record for this book is available from the National Library of Australia

Wakefield Press thanks Coriole Vineyards for continued support

contents

. . . the tree doesn’t know that it’s art

school holidays

the house was small sheltered
by willows along the channel
mud surrounded the milking shed
salt beginning to rise in the paddocks

we sat around the fire reading
until you said *let's go to the creek*
I laughed – *it's almost* bedtime
amazed when your mother agreed

silent paddocks dreamy moonlight
the creek a wide lake of lustrous grey
            in a very wide world
an old rowboat carried us
between ghostly trunks of drowned river gums
the only sound the plip and gurgle of oars
            and the occasional stirring of a bird –
my first night out on water
            under a full moon

after midnight we returned
to your mother still reading Dickens by the fire
            we made cocoa and toast before bed
another midnight first

did I sleep that night
or was the universe too wide?

shock

north-west on the Warakurna road
a substantial mountain range
where no mountain should be

can they possibly break up
drift dissolve in air? my first sight
of a *fata morgana*   named for
King Arthur's shape-changing sister

unlike the pools on the road
when as a kid I followed the sheep
– I knew there could be no water
however real it looked –

unlike when I first saw Aurora Australis
those colourful searchlights beamed
into the night sky   a wild sunset excess

no
the shock is closer to that moment
in Science class
when I learnt my solid desk
            was
                        mostly
                                    space

Pinus radiata

purists would rip them out
they drain the land
destroy the native flora

but the pine on the hillside
immigrant like us
looks settled here

fifteen shrieking black cockatoos
wheel over the myriad eucalypts
to rest in its branches

ingenuity

Jane Paterson in the 1880s
brought a charming purple flowered
plant to her garden

It flourished spread to paddocks
neighbours district southern States
it survived through droughts but
proved toxic to animals

proclaimed a noxious weed
Echium plantagineum was no longer known as
Riverina Bluebell or Purple Viper's Bugloss but
          Paterson's Curse

except in South Australia
ingenuity is required to live in the driest state
farmers learnt to move their flocks onto green leaves
and out before deadly flowering

in this State,
Echium plantagineum is not Paterson's Curse but
          Salvation Jane.

in the Garden

the summers of Hesperides are long
Emily Dickinson

desert dwellers hot and thirsty
wanting water shade and fruit
built gardens with high walls and pools
Hebrews called them Eden –
garden of delight

after the bustle of Rundle Mall
I relax eating grapes
under the giant fig above the lake
memories grow of other rescuing trees:
the peach tree I sat in to read
the claret ash in my mother's garden
the palms shading the beach at Colova
the River Reds fringing Lake Boort
the ancient spreading survivor at my gate

an apartment dweller with pots
          of geranium and basil
my sacred garden is here with lotus
                    plum and bamboo
testament to beauty in simplicity in age
          even with blemish

ripeness is all appeals more
                    as the years mount:
Hesperides summers *are* blissfully long
my thoughts float   the grapes disappear
a boy chasing ducks turns to stroke
                    the velvet leaves of a salvia

Adelaide's own

Fraxinus rotundifolia ssp oxycarpa 'Raywood'

once a random mutation
            in an Adelaide nursery
now planted over half the world
the claret ash in Botanic Park
            bears historic scars

no longer slim and elegant
with every leaf an autumn gem
it holds the large well-rounded shape
of bibulous drinkers in their later years

though the high branches still flaunt
their rich breath-catching merlot
lower leaves remain green or the dun
colour of Penfold's Grange left
                        too long to drink

I gave my mother a claret ash
when in her fifties unwillingly
she followed my father to his farm
carried water in buckets
                        to begin a garden

rare to find such subtle colour beside
the black box and Murray pine
of the Lodden floodplains
thirty years after her death
the ash still decorates
            her abandoned garden
and the heroic display in Botanic Park
                        gives her back to me

Sappho

Rhododendron 'Sappho'
Shiver when Sappho speaks of her Heart Beat. It pounding down through the ages.
Eileen Myles

shiver at this world
of dramatic blossoms:
dark eyes in white faces
inky flares at each heart

strangers debate the central colour
cerise crimson ruby claret?
the poet's love of beauty
pounding down through us

firewheel tree

Stenocarpus sinuatus

red and yellow whorls
shimmy up and down
the gigantic tree
join earth to heaven:

martyred St Catherine
on her fiery wheel
goes home
on Jacob's ladder

this tree
says Margaret Preston
to me
it
doesn't know
that it's art

at St Martin's House

the striking plant in the corner
holds shiny many-fingered leaves
out wide to embrace the room
strong aerial roots take food from air

Monstera deliciosa has many names
commonly the Fruit Salad Plant
sometimes *Locust and Wild Honey*
gruyere plant   ribs of Adam   lion's paw
it's a riot of flavours surprising the tongue

one grew on the tree at our open Suva gate
perforated leaves waved
to the reef's hello

housed in this cliff top retreat
far from your tropical home
where nuns come to recover
and writers search for words

delicious monster of my past
will you ever fruit in this southern
home at the edge of a colder sea?

in transit

so welcome a town in the middle
                                        of endless plains
where pioneer coaches
once rested by the river

sure of a bed at the Cobb Inlander Motel
the traveller strolls along
                              Murrumbidgee banks
past sprawling red gums and noisy corellas

notes how old cottages
                              sit above flood levels
new brick houses risk deluge for views

she returns to her room where a print on the wall
takes her through a white picket gate
to a pale pink cottage surrounded by hollyhocks
under a faded English sky

driving to Boorowa

I've never been a purist
except in the matter of split infinitives
I like
    the vigour of hybrids
        the patchwork of mixtures
            the conjunction of opposites

the casual flock of ibis
reaching for the chalk line
of a jet stream

the row of autumn gold poplars
fronting the patch
    of sombre eucalypts
a homestead called Mulberrygong

reflection

how many monoliths make Uluru?
my photos show red rock
pale sky and climbing moon
Mutitjulu Springs the women's cave
                                        and any painting on rock I find

my friend's photos make collages –
her Uluru is pairs of tourist shoes on the sand
bits of trousers heads from different bodies
cameras raised towards the full moon
over the shoulder of the smoky pink rock
changing every minute as her collages could

tomorrow tourists will take
their versions of earth and moon
to Watarrka and another sunset
to Henbury crater and another film
then to Japan Germany England and Quambatook
to illustrate a thousand different tales

today a ten-year-old walks from the campground
turns her back on Uluru
to take photo after photo of dew on the
leaves of a small ground-hugging plant

Kakadu traveller

beware crocodiles the notice says

the billabong is calm
waterlilies await the arrival
of the lotus bird
dragonflies blue and red
green pigmy geese the perfect couple
a fish plops
mist keeps the exuberant sun at bay
...barramundi for breakfast

birds in the paperbarks
constant as didgeridoos
quivering ground bass of the land

***

across a burnt valley
the pregnant hill is
seeded with caves
where parcels of bones lie
as in the Barrows of Europe

in the sixties Najombolni
added Reckitt's Blue
to his traditional palette
a mother and small son
bodies curved and parallel
float together
in a world of fish

***

the fussy lotus bird
here called the Jesus bird
still walks on the water

pressing the horizon
the sun is a tourist postcard
men fish   women cook
we stroll up the track
with binoculars

the birds sing evensong
as we return in the dark
cook at the easy shared fire
the moon's horns
above the paperbarks
conjure Artemis for us
but here
the moon is a man
the sun a woman
and it is the Mother *'that old lady'*
Kalarrbirri the serpent
who slides through the water
passes into the land

partridge pigeons

approaching
you're in a gangster film
barred vest against bullets
flashy white waistcoat of villains
but the red domino mask
is pure Mardi Gras

contradictory too
the pink and lilac under salesman brown back
the compliant coo coo
and homely waddle as five of you in a line
head for the roadside saloon
disdaining lazy tourists in your path

you are not those patrician birds
who share your name but
live in the high mountains
where brown and white are camouflage
you live in a green world preferring cleared ground
            manage to survive

what bird is that?

As I sd to my
friend (because I am
always talking),—John, I
sd, which was not his
name,
Robert Creeley

white-naped honeyeater
yellow-breasted flycatcher
chestnut-backed button-quail
red wattlebird

forgive me that I have not
named your songs
your bobbing tail
your speckled eggs
your nests delicate or scraggy

am I for you only
a white haired woman?

on returning from China

high above the Megalong
a kestrel
two butterflies around

a stony point
a native pine
in oriental pose

thin trunks of gums
pattern for a screen the
rocks fantastic monsters

fit subjects for an
Emperor's garden
sun glints on dams

in the valley
a farmhouse
huddles under crags

only the sage is missing
and the little boat
which could carry the seeker
toward the distant peaks

at Marlo

the legendary Snowy opens to the sea
tide covers the bar where wading birds rest
a pelican settles near a man cleaning fish
sun dazzles the heath covered dune
                    of my native land

yet a white ibis
on a leafless branch
                    says Japan to me

inland sea

we look from the bus
at a shimmering world
the blue above
swallows all reason

gentle currents have
sculpted the seabed
into red waves
an occasional rift valley

a bore's iron rig
becomes a wrecked galleon
the white heads of Hereford cattle
are mermaids swimming

when the cattle form a queue
at a roadside telephone booth
reality trumps fantasy

mound springs

after a moonscape of salty overflows
five young people from a uranium protest
        nose rings spike haircuts a top hat
dip their toes in the warm water of the Bubbler

gas bubbles rise
        with the slow pulse of jellyfish
to elongate before they burst

sediments lift to a raging circle:
        the giant snake killed by the Arabunna
writhes in its death throes

in silence we watch the pool clear
        wait for the next eruption
from the suffering underworld

pity the monsters Lowell said
        those portents of disaster
that transgress borders frighten us so we kill

the youngsters will return to their protest
        the serpent continues to suffer
will I continue to watch?

parakeelya

Calandrinia balonensis

lovers of solitude
delicate threads sidle through
minute underground tunnels
hunting drops of that rarest gold

above ground
thickened shoots of sober green
prostrate along the ground
waste no energy on show

they hold their tiny gains
against a withering sun
a tensile stem strong enough

to lift against desert gales
a gaudy purple flower:
beauty intended for insects
the hope of continuing life

Torrens Linear Park

newly painted lines on the path
so I'm keeping left up the rise when
a woman rushing to the O-bahn and work
almost collides
no time to see the sun brushing shrubs
the mower doing wheelies
ducks hunting for pools

***

fastidious white ibis in a still river
its top-heavy sickle beak
perfectly suited to the task
white plumed honeyeater
slips off its branch
pretends to be a fantail
big raindrops fall
out of innocuous white clouds
and bikers ring their bells so gently
you don't jump into their path
watch carefully
this could be miracle's day

***

park law: walkers mostly smile often speak
those with dogs are unpredictable
cyclists lower their eyes and accelerate
joggers may grunt depending on age

***

when the honeyeater
hovers to inspect me
I stare right back

***

too wet for strollers this morning
too early for workers
a woman under a purple umbrella
is singing in the rain

Lambert Centre

25° 36' 36.4" South
134° 21' 17.3" East

if butterfly wings in Bolivia
                    affect our weather
what happens to the country
                    when its centre shifts?

once Central Mount Stuart
(named for the Scottish explorer)
rising gracefully two-headed
between those infamous sites
          Barrow Creek and Coniston

now computer men in Brisbane
have done the sums

where the world's oldest river
          meanders into sand and salt
a track leaves the dirt road
near the Aputulas' new dancing ground

no mountains but mulga and dunes
then four metal legs holding
                    a limp wind-battered flag –
the nation's new centre honours a bureaucrat

gathering firewood for our billy tea
we tiptoe round the Lambert Centre
                    careful lest we tilt a continent

rock holes: Mootwingee

reflections boil gently on boulders
the midday sun splits a black gash
through steep walls
drains red from cliffs
cupped around the waterhole

ledges of hop-bush daisies
green grass in a green pool:
it's shrike thrush country
liquid curves of rock and melody

painted hands declare
they tend the Dreaming
for this place

we visit only
since for here
we have no songs

where gorge meets plain
a rusty iron pipe
abandoned homestead walls
bear witness to our stumbles

but on the plains we hear
clear separate pure
the shrike thrush

. . . she sings the song for this place

Mount Wellington

our owners always name us:
for thousands of years
it was Pooranetteri

Montaigne du Plateau
to the mundane French sailor
but he didn't stay

Skiddaw to nostalgic Hayes
for prosaic Matthew Flinders
it became Mount Table

ever hopeful Colonel Sorrell
named it for the famous General
who might repay the compliment

time for change but forward or back?
climbing into a moonscape summit fog
we asked the youngest for a name
I feel spooked she said

the colonisers

the English learnt to colonise on us
the Irish say

first arrive with force
and an extravagant sense of right
take the land and drive out
the inhabitants to the other side
of Shannon Boston or Cooper's Creek

disparage those who remain:
their culture is boorish
their faith idolatrous
their habits lazy lying and thieving

ignore the ancient holy places:
the forts and ditches
the wells and standing stones
where this becomes impossible—
at Navan's great mound or Uluru
make it a money spinner

name *your* sacred sites:
Church Street   Mill Street   Market Street
call your suburbs Brownstown or Redmondville

but the townlands have foiled you –
how to rename sixty-four in one parish?
Auglish Tullylinn Carrickbrack resist
as do Wychitella   Tjukala   Manangatang

fenced land

for the Bicentennial five men on horseback
re-enact Eyre's ride through Nawu country

when he penetrated the land
they now possess and farm

my school history books showed a series of maps
beginning with Australia all black

then a white arc extended from Sydney
a bigger arc after 1813

more white with Sturt Oxley Mitchell and the amazing
Hume'n Hovell before Eyre Leichhardt and Stuart

surprising how much black dissolved
with each explorer's narrow trail

the map has long been uniformly white

when the horsemen repeat Eyre's peninsula rides
his precise route is now impossible to follow

fenced land has lost its music   the Adnyamatana say

the red handkerchief

terrible the silence of the journals

the explorers' anguish sometimes finds words
the cries of the terrified are muffled

searching for water near Mt Deception
Eyre first white man there and his *native boy*

met with a party of native women and children,
but could gain no information from them.

They would not permit me to come near them,
and at last fairly ran away,

leaving at their fire
two young children who could not escape.

he finds two kangaroo skins full of water
as he examines their camp

having taken *some of the water, I tied a red handkerchief*
round one of the children, as payment for it

next day passing the camp he *called to see*
if the children had been taken away

no   still there in the ashes
of the dead fire

They were alarmed when they saw me,
and would take nothing I offered them.

The child around whom I had tied the handkerchief
had managed to get it off and throw it to one side.

Eyre knows he cannot care for them:
decides the parents must return

Under this impression, I put the handkerchief
again around the oldest child, and tying it firmly, I left them.

coming back a fortnight later Baxter checks the camp
to find the children gone   the place abandoned

the red handkerchief of *such fearful enchanters*
left at the camp

and the whole plain around
had been strewn with green boughs

fool's mate

halfway round Fowler's Bay
Eyre camps under many scrubby hills
all of which command our position

uneasy at having *well armed natives*
above him (in spite of their kindness)
he moves camp *to the next hill above them*

they also broke up camp
and took possession
of the next hill

now Eyre moves
to *the highest hill we could find*

final move:
during the day the natives all left

a costly game –
never again would local people guide him

as he searched in misery for water
compelled to drink his horse's blood

Dog Rock Farm

Oolong Creek named for the brolgas
bends to enclose a stage
for those fastidious birds to dance
while dingoes howl on the rocky hill
which later gave the farm its name

lush grasses on alluvial flats
eucalypts and wattles on the slopes
occasional snows flooding down
Ngunawal people passing through

now men come with axe and gun
trees fall brolgas and dingoes vanish
wheat and sheep flourish on the flats
bushrangers and police passing through

Australia Felix

A land so inviting
and still without inhabitants
explorer Mitchell said of the rich Loddon Plains

the inhabitants he couldn't see
yet described as *fine and friendly*
were soon to be driven off
or killed by the diseases my tribe brought
as they rushed stock into a land
so swiftly made infelicitous

within ninety years blown sand buried fences
covered the new ones built on top
dust storms darkened the daylight
carried topsoil to the sea
plates left on tables of abandoned farms

not all the newcomers left –
with better methods   other crops
my hometown flourished
with billiard table paddocks of Loddon water

the Dja Dja Wurrung I never saw as a child
have a presence
defending their culture in court
and a main street memorial honours
the ancestors who never left

there's talk of a treaty

Rye Park Cemetery

the dead long to be of use
read their imposing tombstones
Stop traveller and cast your eye
For as you are so once was I . . .
Be therefore ready . . .

lost babies are everywhere
safe in the arms of Jesus –
children only of their fathers it seems
except for the *child of Miss Palmer*

small plaques have appeared
on unmarked plots –
amongst the Ngunawal families
the Russells the Lewises and Lanes
lie *Aborigine* and *Mary Aborigine*
and in the farthest corner *Old Jack*
we're given our places even here

desert beauty

wide flanks of the mountain range
are topped by deep brown-black rocks
          gabbro
                    I think the geologist said

randomly along the ridge
the skyline is a dragon's backbone
          a mohawk haircut
or where the dark stones spill over
          it's a pudding's chocolate sauce

around the base
          fields of purple mullamulla
bluebells and yellow daisies
          form a delectable coulis

I turn to Tjawina
          with outstretched arms
beautiful country I say
                    in the few words
I know of her language

          yes   she says in mine
                    her grin is wide
lovely one   *plenty emus*

ground bass

in these hills
it is impossible to shout
            the silence folds you in
to a place where
movement is possible
               no clatter of words

if you stay long enough
you hear the breathing of stones and grass
the night hawk's soundless flight at dusk
                    and the surprising winter frost

dancers know this melody
and the woman who whispers in your ear
the story of this place
                           as she lightly holds your arm

the elder

after a meal of thick bread sweet tea
and cold kangaroo tails
the camp quietens   turns to the leader

legs hidden under her black skirt
black beanie on black hair
she sits on bare ground
it’s her land – her gaze goes
far beyond us who wait

she speaks
and everyone moves to prepare
the songs and dances she decrees
painted bodies sway in the firelight
pounding rhythms enfold us
until the songs die away   all is still

the camp flattens into sleeping mounds
                                        between small fires
whose reflections flicker on the mulga
flare as sticks are added
I wake to see the elder lying
 propped on one elbow
Is she listening to her land?
I lie down but not to sleep

no picnic

it's not the Sahara – the green
of cassia wattle grevillea
counterpoints the red dunes
in seductive harmony

yet in this desert
kids weren't named till two
elders too frail to walk
were left at the waterhole
their eyes fixed on the Dreaming.

at Iliatura where figs blacken the water
an Alintjara elder points to the dune
where he found
just bones and bits of check shirt
the man walked miles for bush tobacco
and the waterhole was dry

stories

with digging sticks and hubcap scoops
women are going
for honey ants
I’m thrilled to be invited (so useless)

along the dusty track the senior woman
stirs   leans forward   voice pepper sharp
points to a hillock crowned with quartz
a childhood camp

feet and hands in rhythm
she sings the song for this place
I’m excited
ask for more

silence
the women look away   walk on
my friend touches my arm
it’s a gift   she says   *you receive a gift*

Mount Aloysius

uncompromising
even angular in places
the wide arms of the mountain
remind us of the Jesuit saint
completely uncompromising and angular
who nursed victims of the plague
and died from it

we ask our companion for its name
ini tjuta he says – many names:
for the waterholes at its base
the site of the ancient paintings
the place where Ivy's family sat down
and the ancestral birds rested

the Ngaanyatjarra don't name peaks
but may we add Aloysius to *ini tjuta*
or is it too early?

dance

at sunset
I sit on the ground with the women
among piled up cars broken pipes and bits of tin
            irrelevant backdrop
to this moment when men sweep clear
the dancing place
light a small fire behind the cars
paint their bodies as they sing
            the creation of the world
we who wait are also actors

at a signal I don't know
the women turn away   hide their eyes
order me to follow
one pushes my head to the ground
            hard
her long thin arms so powerful

when I try to lift my shoulders
her hand is heavy again
and again
stays on the back of my head
I'm out of my depth

at a signal I miss
we turn to see the dancers in position
the ancestors' power on chest and face
my neighbour's eyes meet mine
we smile as we straighten
                                    her face is vibrant

sorry

keening swirls around the settlement
the old man is dead
the house of his last breath empty

every possession is burnt
the ground cleared
his family moves to sorry camp

sorry
   sorry
      sorry

the proper people are in charge
must choose the place and time of burial
fax and phone the distant relatives   order planes

his funeral will have Christian words
a wooden coffin takes him to the earth
but the sorry needs a second burial

grey clouds
cold wind
and crows

I'm reading Ginsberg's *Kaddish*
the ancient cry immediate
crossing frontiers
he sees his mother in Russia and Newark
traces her days
speaks her name
she is there

here the old man's name is never spoken
children who share it become *no name*
it blows into the rock and sands of his beginning

caw caw Lord
the crows of *Kaddish* say
and here?

living outside the camp
                                        I can't translate

the community advisor

she's at home in her swag
the creek bed trampled around her
the small circle of ashes   half-burnt stick
signs of a *proper* fire
bird book billy Wet Ones propped against
the food box   shoes upturned on top
she sleeps facing the wind

her body in the swag echoes Skirmish Hill
she's at Moses Creek
upstream is Gosse's Tree where Giles
had trouble with Mr Kanari's grandfathers
they're map names not used around here

other explorers came:
            Lindsay Hahn perhaps Wells
she won't visit – it's men's country
and she is no explorer of the land
her journey is different deeper
walking between cultures so far apart
and (dark shadows around her sleeping eyes)
                        more costly

Darwin's Dog

Irrunytju the dingo is back
she fed him as a pup
thought he'd left for ever

bring him meat
get his rug
he might need water

he sits on her foot his strangled
yowl a conversation
leaves the meat

why has he come if not for food?
surely he's a father now out bush?
perhaps he missed us after all

that night black clouds and wind
thunder a mighty storm
Irrunytju sleeps on his blanket

in the morning he's gone
she checks each track
recalls their desert walks
epiphanies he helped her see

she only offered casual meat
he never was her pet
they always met as equals
both still choose to be free

encounter

Wintjima has run amok   he has a knife
the community is unsettled
the oldies terrified some leave town

the advisor walks toward the boy
sits cross-legged on the ground
empty-handed   *what's the problem?*

he holds the knife at her throat
tell me your problem Wintjima
but first put down the knife

she writes in the sand and waits
the moments pass
onlookers hold a collective breath

then Wintjima throws down the knife
he sits –
and talks

years later when she leaves the lands
the people want for her successor
someone like her – level with us and brave

by the sands of the Todd
I sat down and wept

night falls quickly along the Todd
at 6.30 the light is clear but changing
eucalypts turn to ghosts
the Macdonnell Ranges to purple
a few cyclists and walkers head for home

before 7 it is dark
small fires appear on the dry river bed
as groups gather to drink and argue
loud voices

a man lurches at an approaching woman
pulls her shirt as they tussle and shout
the woman grabs and raises a stick
the shouting grows louder

a young woman overtakes me
dangerous here you go
walks with me past the fractious group
then retraces her steps to join them

and I'm crying

Untyeyetwelye / Anzac Hill

this unpretentious hill
near the centre of town overlooks
buildings bright in the early sun
and the crisp blue of swimming pools

platform for tourist cameras
focussed on the craggy MacDonnells –
tawny ochre or touched with pink
red raw or lilac curtains of mystery

for the Arrente this is the place
where the old Corkwood woman sat
alone needing little no-one

the newcomers honour
a far away battle where men
killed men for no good reason

among broken glass
the climb's first step
has one word written
in yellow blue and white
            SACRED

Mparntwe / Alice Springs

. . . an ordinary street

down by the Lake with Liz and Phil

after Greg Taylor's sculpture, Canberra

dreadful about the Queen and Philip
the woman leaning over the rails
                    interrupts my walk

what's happened?
          someone chopped off her head –
          that naked statue along the lake

uncertain whether execution
or nudity is troubling her
                    I stay silent

the woman walks off mumbling
that someone has stolen
                    her handbag

Bogong song

Mount Nelse North
      is higher
than Mount Nelse

Little Arthur
  overtops
Mount Arthur

Tawonga South's
      a town
of streets and lights

Tawonga just a
    thickening
of the road

the afterthought
        is not
the lesser thought

which

could be some
comfort to
the daughters of Eve

happenstance

if I hadn't double booked the night before
if I hadn't felt guilty at missing a friend's launch
if I hadn't searched frantically for a lost library book
if I hadn't stayed awake all night planning my trip
if I hadn't felt sleepy eyed in the morning dark
if I hadn't encountered thick fog and torrents of rain
if I hadn't kept driving to have coffee at Nhill
I mightn't have nodded off at the wheel
three hundred yards from my planned roadside stop

If I hadn't been in the town's 60km zone
if I hadn't been in a solid low Toyota
if the highway hadn't been clear of cars and trucks
if I'd been deaf and unable to hear the sound
of tyres on the broken edge of the tarmac
or too deeply asleep to feel the change
I mightn't have managed to avoid the post
wrestle the car back onto the road
drive the few yards to the Caltex station
fill up with petrol order coffee
and begin to read a two week old Herald Sun

next morning dull cold and wet
the loveliest dawn I had ever seen

falls

climbing up beside the waterfall
I'm hot sweaty unkempt
easily passed by Japanese women
in neat shorts tank tops
no ruffled hair   no sweat

where from? the valley floor?   I ask
            yes
they may speak excellent English
but I continue slowly *how long?*
they consult splendid Seikos
            hour and a half from the lookout
I'm impressed –

and I am back in Nepal thrilled
to have crossed the Himalayan Pass
when we meet a group of Japanese women
in tight dresses and platform shoes
holding elegant parasols over immaculate hair
 we swagger past gracious and smug
in hiking boots khaki shorts and shirts

our sole Japanese speaker stops to talk
catches us at the next rest house
they're mountaineers off to climb Tutche
a 7000 metre peak in the distance

oh to take back the swagger

chrysanthemums

neat and still stylish
checked by the nurse
            for buttons and stains
she waits in the Resthaven hall
it's taken all morning

in the car she talks and laughs
we're all deaf and blind you know
at dinner Mr Kenny talked
of his gangrenous leg
            soon to be lost
I said your daughter can mend it
            or buy a new pair
I thought he said socks

arriving she braces
slowly lifts and stumbles from the car
            to rest on her white stick
smells eucalypts jasmine
            smoke-drift air of the hills
sees blurred trees against blue sky

across the garden
            a pile of yellow plastic bags
filled with water-saving mulch
            what magnificent chrysanthemums

the old Porsche

the man in the wheelchair is right
                    a perfect day

kids' fluffy clouds in a cobalt sky
          grass newly green
smoky-blue hills frame painted trees
the river idles over stones to reach
          a quiet pool above the weir

a small breeze – a zephyr? –
ruffles the gums heavy
          with rose-red blossoms
I coast over the rise my stride unchanged
          my body purrs like a Porsche

behind me two youths skate down the slope
and a boy's voice breaks the peace
                    watch out old granny

I could stick out my leg to trip him
but resist and delight
                    in such casual grace
hands high on their sun-bleached hair

I wish for them at seventy
a day as rich as this

freedom

sailing from Silesia
to escape persecution
they took willow cuttings
from that river in St Helena
where Napoleon had paced

planted along the Onkaparinga
at a place they called
Valley of Praise
the thriving willows
were woven into baskets
so girls who never knew Silesia
could walk forty kilometres
carrying to market
the fruits of their freedom

Eire

for Mag

I like a country where
their mythological bull
bellows so much in victory
            his heart breaks
where a female champion
            teaches their great hero
and a Fenian warrior must know
            the laws of poetry
and observe the rules of respect

where a stone cries
            at the king's inauguration
where Spanish arrivals
                        burn their boats
where the country is named
            for three women
and the Isle of Happiness
                        is called Mag Mell

the quiet republican

after the service in Tandragee Church of Ireland
I'm invited to tea with an elderly congregation –
            eight women one man and the vicar
I learn of their Australian relatives
see postcards as proof of travels in France

when the tall worried man turns to politics
the air intensifies as all try to explain
their position their sense of betrayal

these Ulster Protestants want my understanding
know the world thinks them wrong
suspect I think them wrong
when they feel supremely right:
one of them said
            it sounds stupid but God is on our side
yet they are so troubled –
            I can offer no comfort

at the door I say goodbye to the vicar
he whispers *I have to be quiet here*
        but I'm for union with the south

I understand his lowered voice
can hardly tell my country town I vote Labor
not even whisper I'm lesbian

how much of Tandragee I wonder
did my great-grandmother bring to me?

art and life

if art's first picture of Virgin and Child
is in the Roman Catacombs
the most intimate must surely be
in Belfast Museum

the Carrickfergus Madonna half smiles
as if knowing how complex the bond

the little boy puts one hand around
her neck under her free-flowing hair
the other rests above her breast

her hands hold his naked body close
long fingers press his thigh his waist

their eyes are inward
mouths a hairsbreadth from touching
they concentrate on contentment

Joseph is out of the picture
a cause perhaps
            of all our endless wars

September 3rd 1939

Sunday evenings Mum goes to church
Dad stays home to talk with his father
but strangely today Dad too goes to church

listening to the new Lux Radio Theatre
my brother and I sit with Grandpa on the couch
still in its winter position in front of the fire

suddenly the producer interrupts the drama
We are at war with Germany
and the play goes on

when our parents return
we remember our news   lift our eyes
We're at war and return to the play

at once Dad strides to the radio
switches to ABC and hears Mr Menzies
repeat his message again and again

no one speaks
the old man and the young miffed
not to hear the end of the play

power again

the day Dad went to war
Mum let the chooks out
just opened the gate
and said *shoo*

that afternoon Mrs Marshall came over
to say our hens had joined hers
              she'd bring them back later

Mrs Marshall please keep them
I'd love you to have them

she'd always hated squawking chooks
feeding   watering   gathering eggs
at Show time Dad washing them
in Reckitt's Blue in her spotless laundry
                    never again

she moved house   sold a house   bought a house
returned to her passion for teaching

rainbow over the Pacific

above the rocky island of Iwo Jima
after heavy cumulus brought cooling showers
a perfect rainbow

how many soldiers and sailors in 1945
saw with lighter hearts such a sight
with its hope of prosperity
and God's guarantee not to drown us all

how many of those from East and West
saw that quick miracle as their last sight
before lowering their eyes again

to the killing fields where
27,000 young men died
fighting over 21 square kilometres
                                        of rock

at the Exhibition

under the title *For Evermore*
two photographers portray
old battlefields in France

one sees rusting iron
the remaining bunkers
blockhouses gun wells
            the bullet holes

the other shows us crops and trees
flourishing above the old trenches
orchards of neat white graves
the tranquil canal where
            Wilfred Owen died

vowels

the English can place you after two syllables
some respond with imperial disdain
most reply with wholehearted friendliness
what part are you from?
Adelaide
a lovely city
have you been?
no
it is a litany
I have an aunt in Sydney

conversation at the Half Moon Inn
began with my vowels
not many patrons at that hour:
a tattooed truck driver whose toddler played
under the sign No Children in the Bar
a young woman in riding gear
and a quiet elderly chap at the far end

we spoke of horses roads and Australia:
the elderly chap told of the kids
sent out during the war
believing they were orphans
thirty years later one came back
and found his parents alive

our friend wasn't sent so far away
only just to York
though it seemed the end of the earth

I was homesick
spent hours and hours making a little perpetual
calendar thing for my mother
much later it came back all broken
and the social worker said your mother's dead.
I never got over it
he could have said I'm sorry your mother's dead

we finished our drinks without a word

Porchester Castle 1950

behind the Roman wall Vespasian built
whose ten feet thickness failed to keep the Saxons out
where young King Hal assembled troops
to sail for France and Agincourt
where bluff King Henry slept with Anne Boleyn
a year before beheading her
where Spitfires overhead kept Germans back
the flannelled boys play cricket

innings ended the batsmen stride
with casually swung bats and deprecatory smiles
the fieldsmen a few steps behind

five girls loll on the grass
skirts tops and open sandals
fair hair loose to their shoulders
interrupt their indefatigable talk
to applaud the returning heroes

today no wartime scars show on young faces –
between grey fort and grey skies   green trees

flight

Incredibly aloof, flinging back the light in a dusky shimmer of bright hair and gilded outspread wings, soared the ranked angels . . . floating face to face uplifted.
Dorothy Sayers: The Nine Tailors

Saint Wendreda's Memorial Church
sits in the hollow of its people's bones
the angel roof saved at the Reformation
by a mighty banquet given to the King's men

bus driver and passengers agree
the famous church is closed for repairs:
the death-watch beetle
keeps me from the angels

the south door is ajar but
my first glance shows a temporary ceiling—
no choirs of angels no seraphim
no *upward sweep of wings*
though one small angel on the wall smiles at me

a recent plaque among the gentry brasses
honours a young Australian pilot
his smiling photo and a faded news-clip
displayed on a table below:

when his bomber caught fire in 1944
the twenty-one year old ordered his crew
to bail out   stayed to wrestle the falling plane
over the village into a field beyond the church
every year his family sends flowers
every day his gift soars above the angels

paradigm shift

home from school
the boy raced to listen
as the workmen yarned of war
                    not Sitiveni –
his bayonet had killed a man
and he had vomited
but war was great for Vili and Joe –
how they tricked the sergeant
stole the rations
drove in convoys through the jungle
still salute each other clicking heels

                    for the boy's tenth birthday
his father sliced bamboo into swords
his mother made bandanas and eye patches
so pirates could fight on the river bank
before the marbled birthday cake

the year the Chief Scout came the young Cub
          slithered over asphalt being Kaa
grazed arms and knees a paltry price to pay
after green uniform   navy blue
garnished with badges stripes and stars
he learnt the perfect head for beer
          at Sea Scout camp

by fourteen he digested books on war
Desert Rats Third Reich A Bridge too Far
anything about his hero Rommel
he planned a coup with fifteen men
        the radio station first then Parliament

a soldier at eighteen with Tarzan ropes real guns
too much exposure to the military mind
at nineteen he left

when children came he changed his work
to do his share of parenting
gently kissing a wounded knee
            teaching his daughters to cook
carrying them on his back to milk Jessie the cow
he wrestles within himself
a system he never chose

amazon

in a quiet corner of the garden
across the lawn from Hebe and Diana
the sun rains gold
on the bare-breasted amazon
astride her bucking horse
a lion tearing its neck

her arm lifts to thrust the lance
only vandals have taken it
and her gaze misses the lion
alights on the duck pond

she has ridden here
since the city was new
while her sisters gallop
through Greece and the world's museums
a fear men never quite forget
a hope too perhaps

this afternoon two women
picnic in the shade of the marble plinth

after a massacre

Hoddle Street

an ordinary street
ignorable
driving thru we
plan the dinner
our strategy for
the meeting
letters we must write
sometimes it's
Forgotten Tunes
or our favourite presenter

we're not ready
for bullets
blood and glass
a war zone

if Hoddle then anywhere
even the Boulevard
a hiccup of fear before
we grill the chops   turn on
death's ever-loving screen

Bali Guest House

nine years she's worked here
seven days a week
from first light till after dark
three children to feed

she brings fresh flowers for the gods
Vishnu preserver maintainer
Brahma   creator source of order
it's clear she favours Vishnu

she places fruit and rice on the altar
with its swastika of harmony
her grace and good humour
the bigger gift

the Mother Temple

high on the slopes of holy Mount Agung
I ride pillion on a motorbike to Besakih
behind a business man of twelve

after last week's festival
the temple is bedraggled
bamboo palisades sag flowers wilt
prayer flags are slivered
the ground scuffed or flattened
but the young guides are all energy
bargain for their fee

returning we reject the scary bikes
walk down the steep slope past stalls
of fruit drinks postcards toilets
Mother Besakih no matter how tired
provides for all her children

the holiness

this cave is temple to the gods
Ishwara Siva Vishnu are stone mounds
but crudely-fashioned Ganesh
keeps his comic temperament

outside the temple six full-breasted
stone women adorned with crowns
hold overflowing water pots
as holy water splashes and flows

nearby a notice warns
with regret that menstruating
women cannot enter the temple
because of *the holiness and our safety*

fish pond

with the precise grace of a temple worshipper
twelve men glide between rice paddies

past bougainvillea poinciana and ginger
fluid as dancing Shiva and as silent

continuous conveyor belt for soil and bricks
they know the hotel fishpond must be ready

for fish to swim past the garden restaurant's
frangipani   glide around volcanic stones

brought from the holy mountain so we visitors
may point to our next meal

for Sappho

because you loved women
stars the moon
gold-sandalled dawn
the shining goddess of the honey bees
bright talk and flowers
and your little daughter Kleis
more than all

because men revered your art
Tenth Muse of honeyed song
because they feared your fame
and burnt your books

because the desert fragments
fill a wide space
we read you still

because we come from lands
where Zeus the thunder god
outroars your golden Cyprian
we must all be poets

plus ça change

Melbourne in the Fifties
tea at Russell Collins
thick carpets   banks of gladioli
I wear a woollen dress and pearls

Frank Roberts in business suit
offers me a job   we talk
I refuse the job
you think like a man Frank says
I am delighted

Adelaide in the Eighties
a drink at Club Foote
black and white   bare boards
I wear my jeans and a scarf

Brooke Watson   pony-tailed
red hat band   reads his long poem
vulnerable   self-aware   wry
Brooke I say *you write like a woman*
is he delighted?

. . . if everything has a name and place

Sans Souci

standing in the circle of his arms
her head reaches his ear as he bends
she smiles at the camera
                                        giving nothing away
he smiles down at her protective proud

teaching or marriage?
             she knows she can't have both
uncertain she moves to another school
                          another town
after a year decides for Bill and Boort

no formal photo of my parents' wedding exists
             only a snapshot as they leave the church
a woman and hat come between
                                        camera and bride
my mother is represented by an elegant leg
                          a fashionable shoe
and a patch of dress I'm told was green

they build a weatherboard and fibro house
they call SANS SOUCI
carefree – they are and hope to be
plan a stained glass panel for the name

when installed in the front door
             it reads SANS SAUCI
they laugh and keep it

shaping

with a hairbrush Mum taps
            my front teeth straight
tries to curl my hair in rags
makes me gargle Condy's crystals
                        against diphtheria
teaches me to read and write
carefully moving the pencil
                        to my right hand

Dad brings back fish from the river
shows me felted goldfinch nests
and the spectacular
                        rainbow bird
teaches me to drive ride shoot
merely regretting that I can't cook
or *entertain a drawing room*

only at tennis do they unite
to coach and cheer proud
when I captain the team
            or win a clock

at eighty-two
I still play tennis

dripping wet

behind the saltbush hedge
I ride my tricycle around the lawn
my mother weeds the rose bed

the gate squeaks open
my young brother stumbles up the path
dripping wet and crying
I called and you didn't come

anger and relief collide in Mum's voice:
            Why did…   Where were…

she gathers him in her arms
bundles him inside to dry –
he'd wandered   fallen into the channel

I sit on the front step
knowing Mum will shake her head
repeat the story with exasperated pride

so this is how envy feels
I'm learning that good girls never attain
the starring roles of wayward boys

first lessons

vivid in the morning sun
red geraniums on the windowsill
taught me left hand from right
if I faced the King's picture

I learnt to worship sitting at the feet
of glorious Miss Edwards
as she pointed to pictures
of **A**apple **B**ball and **C**cat
carefully drawn in coloured chalk

when I copied other kids in Grade 1
carving my initials into the desk
Miss Pedler loomed over me
I expected better of you
a refrain that dogged me through much of life

sitting near the geraniums in Grade 2
I saw Miss Sutherland drop dead in front of us
and Mr Pryor from Grade 6 carry her away

she returned next day
her fainting fit teaching me
the world is chancy

the game

away from the dozing houses
at the top end of our street
the boys play a risky game

one curls into an upright car tyre
with inner tube removed
balances himself with hands held inside

another launches the tyre
to whirl down the hill   wobble
and fall over as the track levels

afraid   yet hoping to belong
I ask for a turn   *you'll have to pass*
a test   it's not for everyone

if you eat a mouthful of dirt you can go
I eat the dirt
the boys run off with the tyre

pomegranate

beside a pomegranate tree in the churchyard
two girls argue over whose father owns the Church –
the Sunday School Teacher or the Minister
          I'm silent
          my father doesn't even go

outside the Greek city of Nafplion
a pomegranate tree guards
                    Hera's sacred spring
where men come in carloads
  to bottle water for their wives to drink:
the goddess promises fertility

no one told us the pomegranate
          was Hera's symbol
or that there were goddess-worshipping days
  before a Father and Son supplanted them
we early learn our mothers don't own churches

sheep

she's only nine but she can work the dogs!
Dad boasts to his mates

sun wind and singing birds for companions
I walk with him along country roads
                              behind the mob
when he returns to the car I'm in charge
but really   I can't control the dogs

today I'm trusted to move the sheep
to the far side of the channel
our faithful dog to help

the sheep baulk at the narrow bridge
                    scatter along the bank
I shout at the dog
          he leaps at the sheep
                    the sheep scatter more
I run one way   dog the other
          herding them back past the bridge
                              again and again
hot exhausted crying   I'm alone in the universe

a miracle: one sheep ventures onto the bridge
another follows
                    cautiously a few more
I hold my breath
          the rest saunter across into the paddock
the dog smug as if it's his success
I rush to shut the gate
          throw myself under a tree

Dad keeps boasting of his daughter

red blossoms

I see you walking your hard-won farm
from native pines and mallee sands
in the cleared paddocks
          to red gums on the creek
and the crab-holed black box plains
                    around the lake

do you hear sounds below the birdsong
as you take visitors to see
                    the canoe tree's scar?
you dig into middens for the farm tracks
          great stuff for boggy country

can you see people behind
                    the grey-green canopies
          who called this place *Le-aar-ghur:*
red blossoms or the bleeding tooth
the colour's red whichever

I buy red poppies on Remembrance Day

revelation

I fashioned a tragic figure of you
not from your hilarious tales
but with bones from your sister's stories
flesh from my own flawed view –

a toddler hiding from your drunken father
bright scholar leaving school at thirteen
alone in town with that pitiable father
your beloved mother's long illness
the hard Depression years

cost of war to you old soldier
an eye and a brother left in the jungle
the guilt of leaving your men behind
a ten-year struggle to breathe
huge nightmare fireballs coming again

when cancer came you seemed resigned
an extra thirty years you said
thinking of your brother Hal
Smithy Frank and half the regiment

in drama class one night I acted you
hitched up my pants
pushed the hat back on my head
whistled the border collie to my side
and sauntered behind the sheep

lost in each flowering bush and tree
each nesting zebra finch
the colours of a rainbow bird

meeting

twenty years
after his death
he comes towards me
on the path

grey hair
military walk
same tentative
carriage of the head

for a millisecond
I start to run to him
wish I had
when I could

tracing the genes

after the jam factory fruit picking
ward-cleaning dishwashing student days
my first real job – agriculture department:
plant breeding section
                                        geneticist grade six

no ethical concerns hampered me
a bungling beginner in the new age
                         of genetic modification in the lab
I tried to induce mutations by shaking up
             chromosomes with chemicals

having failed to produce anything of value
                                        (read commercial)
I left to begin my own breeding plan
where each arriving specimen is priceless

perhaps that early work spurred
                                        the pursuit of my clan
the frustrated scientist finding it easier
                                        to trace the genes back
than design them for the future

equation

how to compute
the *equation of days*
is a problem
not only for sundials

is a day strolling
the paths of my ancestor's country
equal to one searching for a farm
in the Tithe Apportionment Maps?

what can be added to a day
reading wills in Lewes
to equal time alongside
the Medway at Hartfield?

what magical measure can equate
long hours in a stationary bus
with the time of a lover's kiss
a friend's call
a grandchild's match-winning goal?

headland

jutting into the channel
North Foreland separates Broadstairs
from Margate –
these magnets for summer trippers
who come in driving rain or fitful sun

a lolly shop with glass jars to the ceiling
a fish and chip shop with plastic tablecloths
and icecream sundaes in silver bowls
a beach beside a grey and choppy sea –
sufficient paradise

my ancestor Sarah would have seen it
differently: as the ship
turned into rougher waters of the Channel
most of them were seasick
the surgeon wrote of his cargo

standing in the rain on the grey shore
a striped lolly bag safe under my umbrella
I look out across the waves
                                        for a small ship

on board a tough little Sussex woman
sails past me towards our future

lullaby

what do you bring from Ireland
when you leave at seventeen?
my great grandmother Lizzie carried fine linen
            for her wedding dress
and her mother's lullaby

bye o bye o dear little baby

she sang it to her children
in a tent on the Ballarat goldfields
then in a small house near the mine at Whim Holes

her daughter Sarah sang it to my mother
as they travelled around Victoria
singing the Lord's songs

my mother sang it me in a small lakeside town
when the fierce Truby King decreed
we should lie screaming for our four-hourly feed

she is such a darling baby

I walked the midnight floor
crooning it to my children
to the rustle of tropic palms

my daughter sang it to her children
in the cool beauty of the Adelaide Hills

now that young woman sings it to her daughter
along with lullabies in Italian and French
as the sands of the desert blow

What next for this Irish tune?

enough

A rare opportunity is here presented for the emigration of respectable single females to Victoria. …as successful diggers usually get married as soon as circumstances permit, the few women who arrive are usually soon removed from servitude.
Armagh Guardian, Nov–Dec, 1852

the promised husbands were not
where the anchor dropped
not on the lighters taking them
across the bay to Geelong
not at the pier nor on the wagons
carrying them uphill to the depot
or if they were
the young girls didn't know

first they must pay for their passage
in floors scrubbed
cows milked   meals cooked
and babies soothed
domiciliary servants to their sponsors
sometimes more

my great-grandmother Lizzie was fortunate
two months after she was free
the husband appeared
she stopped him in the street to ask directions
twenty years older but admitting to ten
a Londoner who made top hats
and went to her church
that was enough

mad

Kenmore Hospital Cemetery

the man in the office is embarrassed when
I ask to see my great-grandmother's grave
            we're going to fix the cemetery
I'm taken across several paddocks to a small
unkempt area hidden by pines

there are hollows amongst ordered rows
of unnamed wooden pegs
is Caroline here?
Oh no he says *these are Japanese soldiers*
this was a military hospital in the war

Not Cowra? there the Japanese war dead
lie in precision rows beside cryptomeria
planted by the Emperor's sons
an altar to ease the warrior's passage
It's different he says *these soldiers were mad*

somewhere beyond the pines
under tall thistles and weeds
lies Caroline
victim of a different war

the Mitchells

I'm one of the Mitchells
Les Murray

preparing for a broadcast my friend reads
the line four ways I try it then use my name
the one I took on marriage: I'm one of the...
suddenly I see again my maternal graves
under a Sussex yew beside a Norfolk tower
in Canberra Ballarat and Geelong

my mother's grave bears her husband's name
her family links not acknowledged:
Southwell Freeman
Turk Haines Brown Wimble and Woodland
and hundreds more

I'm not one of my husband's tribe
as he is not of mine I have no links
with Rochdale or Box Hill
and any name I use from now
must be my own

belonging

is it a black-chinned honeyeater
          or merely a white-naped?
which species of eucalypt?
where is my grandparents' house?

why this passion to name
to recognise
          to place

I have spent hours bent over
          old records
to discover whether my ancestors
worked on the Cobbitty properties
          of Matavi or Denbigh
– wanting it to be Matavai
a link to my South Pacific past

perhaps I am hoping that
if everything has a name and place
so might I

. . . what if love is tensile threads

Kamotu

Kamotu we called her
the little blue boat
pet name Salote gave
our daughter years ago

what diamond seas we sailed
what bays we explored
the picnics the races
the long homeward glide
now she lies beached
out of reach of the tide

oh mariner my darling
mend the boat
sail into these various seas
the waves are tempestuous
rips currents divide
yet the deeps wait   still and alive
sail sail your sturdy boat then dive

long marriage

he feeds a currawong at their picnic spot
she protests
hates its demanding eye   cold confidence
impervious to dislike

two bits of biscuit he throws
the currawong   head tilted   inspects and swallows
a third and more
each time the inspection   pause   swallow
another and another
each time the bird comes closer

that's all   he says sipping tea
closer now the currawong
inspects a biscuit-like pebble
clacks it shakes it and swallows

see what you've done she says *it could die*
having attained the high ground
she settles to enjoy her tea

break

divorce
and a husband of thirty years
becomes a brother

who fixes my taps
shares parenting (now grand)
sometimes a house

incomplete fracture
our psychiatrist friend
had warned

as if we're arms and kneecaps
marriage embodied
in our drained bones

what if loving is tensile threads
which need not hamper
do not break?

ten years on
our friend
sits with us at breakfast
says *your life is to be envied*

my tiny flick of triumph fades:
next week unknown
today the coffee is strong and good

Browns Beach

was he a farmer of this arid
                    limestone soil
a fisherman trawling this prolific sea
perhaps a City man
          come to forget his desk
could a Mary Brown be honoured here?

two kangaroos watch in curious unconcern
as we unpack the car   put up the tent
once married now apart
                    we know each other's ways
who will unroll the bedding
who prepare the meal

he's borrowed our son's sleeping bag
the name their name is stencilled
                              on the cover

no longer labelled for father or spouse
I've chosen to keep my given names
as flags on a ship send messages to port

phylogeny

each day she changes
the first gurgle
          first smile
                    first sit and crawl
then the lurch around a coffee table
holding with both hands
                                        then one
until she stands unaided
claps her hands
                    with the same glee
as her ancestors
climbing out of the trees
to stand erect
          on the plains of Africa

Claire   on her baptism

clear mountain creeks and deep pools
your slow smile begins in quiet
                    and overtakes you
your forehead wrinkled
                    yet some sense of calm

two robust streams meet in you
                    the talkative Irish
great celebrators of everyday
                    providers of pubs in desert places
the sturdy Methodists
                    save for the odd rebellious drunk
sang Wesley's hymns with gusto
                    built chapels on their land

today another stream's acknowledged
                    spires and aspirations
St Francis and St Clare
                    poverty and ecstasy
your mother and two godmothers bring you to the priest
                    promise a family of faith

a believer in living
                    I kiss your forehead
smile into warm eyes
                    halfway to lively brown
and wish for you clarity content
and just sufficient turbulence to make the ocean home

pianist

serious at the piano
my young granddaughter
lifts her hands from the keys
turns with a grave achieving smile

my chest tightens
as when her mother's first
toothless grin induced in me
a complicated joy

I swear to ban all weapons
heal every wounded soul
fight every evil scheme
so she may live in safety

unhurried in the kitchen
her father calls us back to tea

blue rug

for Robin

your sister hauls you by the head
we leap to rescue you
place you on your own blue rug
a quiet sea?   a cloudless sky?

four robins were appliqued with care
scarlet yellow hooded and pink
the back is rainbow dots on white
party boy?   searcher of the skies?

naked you lie soft and open
your smile is easy
your father and his friends explore a way
to be both vulnerable and strong

born in the misty hills above the city
and already a desert traveller
what further journeys will you make?
into what world?   what man become?

wisdom

i

in the hills a four-year-old loves princesses
especially Cinderella *so beautiful*

her mother knows her duty:
    it's not appearances that count
    but what you're like inside

the kid nods dark pony tail bobbing
    bones she says

ii

red and yellow cloak flying
Superman is running
his three year old legs pumping
he's singing my god running
flat out and singing
until he reaches the foot-bridge
with its broken plank
to sit gazing as the water streams below
Superman overcome

iii

brown eyes shine like sunset lakes
brown hair frames a pixie face
at six she sees no need for school
I can read and write already!

the nuns told her Methuselah
lived to be a thousand
what do you think? she asks
    you first what do you think?
ridiculous

clouds

from *"Both Sides Now"* by Joni Mitchell

I've looked at life from both sides now
two friends at the piano
the big woman with flowing hair and caftan
the schoolgirl in plaits and pastel uniform
the rich mezzo of the trained singer
the clear tones of the child
unequal but blending
they laugh at their mistakes
begin again when the songbook falls

I've looked at love from both sides now
they sing for the woman on the couch
a birthday gift
tears prick as she looks through open doors
and the always open gate
to the lagoon restless under the wind
music is the weather of this house

it's cloud illusions I recall
clouds are building over the reef
white and grey-blue edged with black
heavy   powerful   in constant change
soon all three women will leave this harbour
the moment taken with them

touch

so cuddly at two
you grew long legs and a long frame

so gentle at fifteen
you stretched alongside me on the bed

seeing Freud's accusing eyes I panicked
pushed you off

two years later you were in the Army
was I to blame?

today I sit on the grass talking
you come past looking for your child

touch with your finger the crown of my head
rub for a second and walk on

I look at your long back and the careful way
you bend your knees to walk uneven ground

and that cord cut thirty years ago
knots and tightens

Willis Biddi with Louise

such white rocks in the Snowy –
backbones of submerged dragons
diprotodon teeth
sunshine shadows the mystery rock
it's Lou's place

she brings two cups of mountain water
unspilt over slippery stones
I tell the story of King David in battle
longing to drink *of the well at Bethlehem's gate*
three young warriors broke through
enemy lines to bring the water
which the king poured on the ground –
a libation too sacred to drink
silly bugger she says

she shows me where
the strange men camped
and she hurried away
she picks up an ancient microlith
for me to admire
then carefully replaces it

I take as gift an emu feather light and strong
and a stone egg
earth-coloured river-smoothed
a tiny chip against perfection
portrait of my friend

Emily for breakfast

my friend Sue laughed when
I said I had Emily for breakfast
but she does nourish me

in my twenties with less time to read
it might have been theology I tried
          Niebuhr perhaps or Barth

by my thirties probably a Fijian Grammar
          written by my friend George

forties fifties and sixties
Germaine Marge Piercy and Adrienne

now I turn to the profound American
poet who seldom ventured
from her haven behind the hedge
yet speaks to the world
          and to me

for Kay at fifty

got your keys? we say as one
and laugh – we mothers know
the quirks of that much-examined role
but so much more than mothers
on this perfect summer's day
which ends our year and your decade

we walk so easily together
talk books ideas events and body pains
sharing the spotlight on such different lives
equally engrossed in the cockatoo's slow climb
on the mottled trunk of a river gum

we're both writers: know the unsatisfied
quest for simplicity and shape
have learnt truth can't be cornered
yet search for partial truths
on which to bet our lives

now that I've met your aunts I see
your quick energy as Pittsburgh given
tempered in Bathurst and Taperoo
but vision and perseverance
warmth and openness are your own
more than enough for Adelaide and your fifties

the salute

in Resthaven's functional dining room
two women sit silent
comfortable together   minds intact

an aide sweeps up cups and plates
leaves for shaking hands
two mounds of pills

a stooped woman as she passes by
intones *I'll die tonight*
the friends exchange wry smiles

set themselves to stand
manage on the second try
and reach for metal walking frames

salute each other with raised hands
as cavaliers riding to battle
or climbers below the summit

begin the slow plod down corridors
to white-sheeted loneliness
waking next morning
to their constant Everest

walking the trail

on my fifty-ninth birthday
I sleep in the open
Wilpena Pound a firm mattress
my friend's generous body
a bridge to comfort

the sun sets over the rim
in Aries
as we eat flat bread and peanut butter
no fires allowed
we're in our feathered wombs by seven

three native pines
hold Christmas fingers to the stars
but it's the wobbly Easter moon
rising in Virgo
who lurches over the eastern rim
to silver the autumn grasses
smile on four sleeping women

I too am smiling
we have a long walk ahead
through Dreamtime splendour:
Woodnawolpina Buninyunna
Umberatna Moralana Wonaka
the sun will wake us warm
though frost covers our bags
and in our packs   still
oranges for breakfast

the phone box

I'm in an unfamiliar part of town
flat grey land between city and sea
piers ahead lift rusting metal to the clouds

now empty they were once the gateway out
where bright girls set off with streamers
and the fumes of H deck
for the ritual journey Home – dishwashing
in the Strand then Eurail pass to Venice

and my bright girl forbidden lover
one of them

the day before she sailed we walked the decks
glanced quickly at the narrow berth
where she would sleep alone
and left
silent and walking apart
until we pressed into a phone box for one last kiss
before the green bus came and rattled us to town

I stayed while she stepped off   turned
for one last look   one frozen wave
before the bus lurched on

I have spent the years since then
shoring my life against such desolation

pelicans

the pelicans glide in the hot sun
settle in the water
like the Air Force Sunderlands
at Laucala Bay

thirty years ago
we watched those big birds
lumber from water to air
our bodies electric with constrained passion

we took off on different flight paths
now
seven children two husbands
how many lovers later
we sit in canvas chairs outside the tent
our washing sails on the paperbarks
you bring a drink
our bodies touch in easy knowing
as the pelicans glide from air to water
in the afternoon sun

the walls of Lesbos

to build a Lesbian wall
take big rough stones

don't cut to fit
they are themselves undressed

balance each with care
use no cement   no force

large gaps remain
the strength is in the touching
            and the spaces

long knowing

when you make a sandwich
I know how you'll hold the knife
spread butter into each corner
pat the tomato into place

when you drive a car
I know when you'll turn the key
adjust the seat and mirrors
pull at the straining belt

when you touch a face
I know how your thumbs roll out
the way you press your fingertips
the long and gentle strokes

I know the way you argue:
refuse to let me walk away
offer a pillow or baseball bat
persist until we're clear

when I trust you with my
wild uncertain depths
I never know what oceans we will reach
you keep your mystery still

good night

dark cupboard in the corner   door shut
the little girl in the back bedroom
lies rigid
eyes stare at the window where monsters
come through the quince tree to enter
she turns to the wall for relief
but cannot stay
she must remain on watch

forty years on my friend tucks me in bed
settles pillows at my side
softly strokes my face
lights a candle by my bed
then leaves
the faint sweet smell of beeswax
the warm glow of the tiny flame
fills the room
the little girl's ancient fear uncurls
she turns to the wall   smiles
and sleeps

aventurine

naked and large against the horizon
you lean into the waves
lifting your arms to bless the arriving waters
more Willendorf than Venus on her shell

we're travelling women:
have shared so many journeys
in my house your house our house
in green tent grey tent and azure blue
in motels hotels cabins and under the sky
remember we made it over the Himalayan Pass
that dawn with sun and moon bright
that Great Wall we trod which kept no-one out
those powerful Henge stones on Salisbury Plain
the dozens of engraved vulvas on Carnarvon Gorge –
the plaque said *significance unknown*

our present dreams pull us apart
a continent will lie between
but space need not mean distance
in my bag lie two green stones
sea-smooth *aventurine*
we'll take one each:
they may lie close again
and we may swim together
in the constantly returning waters

Mother's Day

white chrysanthemums
in plastic buckets
star the pavements
our annual celebration of guilt

lover
I bring a yellow rose
for celebration
in our world it says
I am available to you

it's barely true
ghosts past and future
beguile distract
demand

yet still I'm here
woman coming to woman
nourished nourishing

in fantasy
I see you in a cave
forming yourself from rock:
pillowed belly of sandstone
sea-pastured
satin flesh of heavy breasts
tongue-crying coils of nipple
earth-coloured steady eyes
mother figure for the unmothered

you smile a deliberate welcome

will you be here for me always? I ask
knowing the answer is no and yes

miracle

she stops at the plum tree
leans on her elbow crutches
head forward to inspect the rough branch
so heavily pruned this year

she calls me   waves her crutch:
a tiny green shoot is pushing
through tough old cambium
how can such soft tissue survive?

soon tiny leaves and stronger twigs will follow
then blossom perhaps even fruit this year
another miracle – her step almost jaunty
as her sticks take her to the car

Karen

her photographer's eye
saw the world –
and loved it
without reading the books
she knew that *this is*
is what there is
and this is enough

Acknowledgements

Miriel completed the manuscript of *driving to Mulberrygong* before her death, but had not written the acknowledgements that we know she would have wanted to include. She was always warm in her appreciation of the contributions and support given by her writing companions and friends.

For this book, Miriel would have wanted to acknowledge and thank particularly Margaret Merrilees and Jill Golden for their huge commitment and contribution to the selection of poems and preparation of the book; also Sue King and Caroline Bamford for their help with typing and final edits of the manuscript; Louise Crisp for her insights and feedback, and Robin Parkin for his ideas and cover design.

Ruth Raintree, sounding board and help through all of Miriel's books, died a few months after Miriel and we would like to acknowledge her invaluable contribution to the preparation of *driving to Mulberrygong*.

Diwani Oak created the painting for the cover and we are very grateful to Diwani for her beautiful work.

Sincere thanks to Diane Fahey for her endorsement.

Finally, our gratitude goes to Michael Bollen and the team at Wakefield Press for their work in producing another fine book for Miriel's final collection.

www.ingramcontent.com/pod-product-compliance
Ingram Content Group Australia Pty Ltd
76 Discovery Rd, Dandenong South VIC 3175, AU
AUHW021252180725
414048AU00002B/2

9 781923 388031